TOM HEGNA'S

WHO WANTS TO *Be a* MILLIONAIRE?

BY TOM HEGNA

Contents

Foreword 1

Preface 3

Introduction 9

Chapter 1: "I Help People Become Millionaires" 15

Chapter 2: The 3 Phases of Wealth.. 21

Chapter 3: Financial Wellness Defined 33

Chapter 4: Saving and Investing for Retirement..................... 39

Chapter 5: A Few Words about Debt 51

Chapter 6: Advisors who "Get it." 55

Chapter 7: Where are YOU on the Mountain? 65

Chapter 8: A Little More About Life Insurance........................ 73

Chapter 9: Building Wealth 81

Chapter 10: Financial Wellness and Health are Related. 89

Chapter 11: Taxes are Headed Higher!................................... 93

Chapter 12: Some Tips from Curtis Cloke 99

Chapter 13: Final Thoughts 105

About the Author 107

Foreword

As someone who has spent their entire life in the insurance industry and helped numerous professionals with 3,000+ training videos, hosted conferences of 2,000+ attendees, and created the industry's first ever reality show called The Ultimate Agent, I cannot emphasize enough how excited I am about this book. The timing of its release could not be better. It is a breath of fresh air in a market that is full of outdated information, and I am confident that it will change your life.

I'm so excited for you to read it, take notes, and apply its principles. I just finished it, and it is truly remarkable. I encourage you to read every single word. I first heard of Tom Hegna from my father back before I even started in the insurance industry. Ever since I've been a complete sponge with everything he's ever released. He's been such a huge blessing in my life, back before he even knew it, and he's about to be a huge blessing in your life (if he hasn't already).

I remember a few years back when our agency was considering hiring Tom for our local annual agency event in Springfield, Mo. To say I was excited about the opportunity to finally meet Tom would be an understatement. As he always does, he showed up and delivered an incredible talk about insurance's power, the importance of growing your money, and how those two are a perfect match.

He was generous with his time as he hung around for what felt like an hour and just spoke with me about what I was doing, which conferences I should want to speak at, and advice on how to grow my own thing. This moment lit a fire in me, and to this day, he doesn't realize how much this moment truly meant to me. I can tell you this, anytime I can get around, spend time with or learn from Tom, I jump at it, and you should as well. He's a true titan and legend in our space.

He paved the way for us young guys to continue to advance the greatest industry on the planet. I don't believe anyone has done more to love our industry so far. He's all about teaching and giving back. What he is about to teach you in this book will change the way you think about and see money for the rest of your life. When it comes to our industry, the financial industry, which has produced the most millionaires of any industry, and when it comes to teaching you the fundamentals of growing money and becoming a millionaire... the most qualified person on the planet who is an absolute expert on this topic is none other than... TOM HEGNA.

By Cody Askins

Preface

any of you know I have spent my whole career focused on helping retirees retire the optimal way. In fact, I have written 5 books on the subject – 3 for American retirees and 2 for Canadian retirees. But this book is not about retirement, it focuses on helping young people become wealthy so someday, they can retire too.

I have always encouraged people to "stay in their lane." That means know what you are good at and keep doing that. Don't try to be everything to everybody. Stay focused on what you are an expert at. So, am I deviating from my own advice? I hope not. I really think I can help young people think about money differently. This is the same advice I have used in my personal life and the advice that I have shared with my own children.

How did this book come about, anyway?

It's an interesting story. In 2022, I was asked by a couple of Fortune 500 insurance companies to build a presentation on financial wellness. Financial wellness is currently a buzzword in our industry. Many people are concerned that Americans are not being taught how to handle money properly. In the past, your parents and grandparents didn't really need to be sophisticated investors because they received guaranteed income for life in the form of pensions. Today, with 401k's and IRA's, that responsibility has been transferred to the individual.

I had to do a lot of new research since it doesn't just deal with retirement. It deals with debt, housing choices, saving, investing, funding college and so much more. I was shocked to see how closely financial wellness is tied to physical wellness, emotional wellness, and mental wellness.

It is interesting to see how many people struggle with these issues. CNBC said in January 2023, that 64% of Americans are living paycheck to paycheck. Market Watch just came out with an article stating that more than half of Americans who make over $100,000 are living paycheck to paycheck as well. That is crazy! Why is it happening? Because people are making bad choices with their finances.

I know, I know, it's not their fault. It's the fault of the government, or billionaires, or inflation or large corporations or 100 other excuses. Sorry, but that is what they are: excuses. Do you know how I know they are excuses? Because plenty of people, at ALL income levels, are saving, investing, and retiring happy. They don't make excuses. They plan and then execute that plan.

That is what I want to do with this book. I want to give you SIMPLE, EXECUTIBLE steps to become wealthy. I will also show you how simple it is to avoid many of the problems (since many problems are self-inflicted). When I say simple, that is what I mean. My office once made a social media post saying it was "easy" to become a millionaire. I made them take it down. It is not easy, but it *is* simple.

I'm a golfer. I like to use golf as an analogy to explain this. Investing is a lot like the game of golf! Both investing and golf are very simple.

There are 3 phases in golf:

1. The tee shot
2. The approach
3. The putt

In investing, there are ALSO 3 phases:

1. Building wealth
2. Protecting wealth
3. Distributing wealth

In investing, we can't use the same products for all the different phases. Wealth building products won't help protect wealth. Wealth distribution products won't help build wealth.

In golf, I'm allowed to carry 14 clubs. I don't use my lob wedge to tee off on a par 5. That wouldn't work well! I don't use my driver out of a sand trap. I don't use my putter from 150 yards out.

Each club is a product with its own function.

And it's the same with financial products.

I find too many financial advisors who are not using all of the clubs in their bag.

They only want to sell managed money.

They only want to sell annuities.

They don't want to sell life insurance.

When it comes to building wealth – mutual funds, annuities, managed money, and life insurance can do that. Building wealth with disability insurance or putting your money into long term care insurance won't work.

When it comes to protecting your wealth, annuities, life insurance, and disability insurance will work, but managed money, mutual funds, and stocks and bonds won't. An investment product can't make up wages if someone is disabled. Millions of dollars are at risk without high liability limits and an umbrella policy.

Life insurance provides tax free income in retirement.

When it comes to distributing wealth, managed money isn't going to distribute wealth efficiently – that's what annuities do. Life insurance provides tax free income in retirement.

So what I'm saying is: Each club in my bag has a different function, and I don't use the wrong club in the wrong situation.

It's the same in financial services.

Use the right product in the right situation. You don't want an advisor who says, "I'm just going to carry a 7 iron."

A 7 iron isn't going to get you a good score if that's ALL you carry! Use all the products in the bag.

See, golf is a very simple game. But it is certainly not easy! It's the same with becoming a Millionaire. I will share very simple concepts that will make you wealthy. However, implementing the concepts will require discipline, patience, and persistence.

Anyway, financial wellness just sounded boring to me. So, I changed the title to *Who Wants to be a Millionaire?* About this time, Jeremiah Desmarais of Advisorist reached out to me. He was having a huge virtual financial advisor summit and was seeing if I wanted to be a part of it. There was no money in it, but there would be several thousand attendees. I wanted to try out this new material anyway, so I said, *"Sure, I'd love to do it."*

The rest is history. I presented these concepts in the form of a webinar. The webinar went great, and we increased our followers by thousands. Jeremiah and I have done a number of meetings together in the past. We just seem to click. He shows advisors how to fill their calendars with qualified appointments, and I show them how to explain these concepts to their clients and prospects—kind of like peanut butter and jelly (or ham and eggs).

After the Virtual Financial Advisor Summit, Jeremiah called me and asked me if I had ever thought of turning this presentation into a book and showing people how to build wealth. I said I was indeed working on a new book, but it was not based on that presentation. The more I thought about it, the more Jeremiah's idea made sense to me. So, here we are!

This book is not complicated. It should be a quick read as well. But the information is very powerful if put to practice. So please, use a highlighter or take notes on the key areas that you can implement to ensure that you too can have a wonderful and exciting retirement in the future. That is really what it is all about.

Introduction

You don't get to take any money with you when you leave this world. But that doesn't mean money is not important. You need money for almost all aspects of your life. I will show you how to make more, spend wiser and put your money into places that will help it grow.

Although I will discuss the 3 phases of wealth: Building Wealth, Protecting Wealth and Distributing Wealth, this book clearly focuses on the first phase: Building Wealth. I get some haters who say, "Tom, a million dollars is nowhere near enough in today's world, and it will mean almost nothing in 25 years." I don't disagree.

But let me tell you from experience, the first million takes the longest and is the hardest to attain. Once you get a million, it is much easier to turn that into 2, 3, 4 million or more. It reminds me of when I was in the Army ROTC program at North Dakota State University in 1983. We had an assignment to write a paper on why we wanted to become a 2nd Lieutenant in the US Army.

I wrote that I didn't want to be a 2nd Lieutenant. I wanted to be a General, but the Army doesn't hire Generals. I thought it was cute, but the Major in charge of the class didn't like my sense of humor. A million dollars shouldn't be your final goal, think of it as more of a first step towards financial independence. Hundreds of millions of Americans will never reach that level. I don't want you to be part of that group. I want to welcome you to the group that millions of other Americans are in – the group of millionaires!

I also want to acknowledge that financial wealth is hardly the only measure of total wealth. Your health, your family, your peace of mind, or your happiness may be even more important. I'm not a doctor, a psychologist, a pastor, or a psychiatrist. I write and speak about financial matters. So that will be the focus of this book.

Ask anyone, having money helps you be healthier, and hopefully happier!

Ask anyone: having money helps you be healthier and hopefully happier! Plus, having money allows you to help others – the poor, your church, your university, your family. If you don't care about money for yourself, this book will help you give more to others.

Some of the concepts I will be sharing, you might already know – the rule of 72, the time value of money, opportunity costs, etcetera. However, I will try to show them in a way that really makes them come to life. Remember, back in the 80's, I was a Financial Advisor with MetLife. I learned pretty quickly that most people don't know many of the things I had studied and learned about money.

I found myself spending most of my appointments teaching and coaching rather than selling products or designing detailed financial plans. Much of what I was doing was delivering basic financial education. My clients sincerely appreciated that I was focused on them fully understanding the WHY behind my recommendations.

Further, I would carry my own financial documents to show them that this is where I put my money as well. My entire career I have walked the walk, not just talked the talk. How could I ever think about selling a million dollar or 5-million-dollar life insurance policy if I didn't own one myself? How could I recommend mutual funds, annuities, or any other investment if I didn't also have my money there?

There is a lot of babble about the Fiduciary Standard and compliance. I have seen more than a few advisors claiming to be Fiduciaries who every day do NOT act in their clients' best interests. They refuse to protect retirees from the many risks in retirement. They refuse to recommend insurance products to their clients. These "fake fiduciaries" will have their comeuppance soon enough.

I used a very, very simple fiduciary standard. If I would not do it for myself, if I would not recommend it to my mom, dad, or my sisters, I would not recommend it to a client or prospect. That was it. And following that simple standard has served me well for the past 35 years. There will always be bad financial advisors out there. But the good ones outnumber the bad ones and I absolutely believe you need to work with a financial advisor. You don't do your own dental work in your garage, and I don't think you should do your own financial planning.

This book will show you that ALL of you will earn millions of dollars over your lifetime. The real question will be "how much will you KEEP?" I'm going to show you how to keep more.

I will also go over the many roadblocks that will trip up many of your peers. Many of them won't have a plan. How can you ever know where you are headed if you don't have a map, GPS, or a plan? Think of a financial plan as your financial GPS. They will forget about inflation. That a million dollars today will be worth much less in the future.

They won't have an emergency fund. When the car breaks down or the air conditioner dies, they will need to steal from their retirement funds. They will procrastinate. They will keep saying "I'll do it next year."

They won't realize how much taxes are going to have to go up in the future. When the government takes 50% or 60% of their 401(k) in retirement, they will feel victimized and blindsided. They will continue to rob their future by spending way too much on their cars. This section of the book, alone, can change your financial future.

Over half of your peers will get divorced. This can devastate both partners' financial future. They will be paralyzed by all the competing priorities – we want a new car, a new house, to send our kids to a nice college—oh yeah, that retirement thing is important but it's going to have to wait.

But not you! You are going to learn how to make more money. You are going to find your IKIGAI! You will find your niche because there are "riches in niches!' You are going to have the answers to attaining the level of wealth you desire.

The book will conclude with some very simple, executable steps that will put you solidly on the track to a wealthy future. Again, these are same steps that I have used and shared with my family. You should know that for 30 years; I spent over 200 days a year on the road. I was the hardest worker I knew. My family sacrificed – I missed birthdays, anniversaries, ballgames, even some funerals of my extended family. It was hard.

But I kept remembering the quote "If you are willing to do the things other people are unwilling to do, eventually you will be able to live the life few can live." I am writing this aboard the Emerald Princess on a Panama Canal Cruise. I am now in a very different stage of my life.

I am no longer focused on earning money. I am focused on living life! My finances now allow me to live an incredible life. None of us knows how many more days we have; I am focused on getting the most out of life and helping as many people as possible.

Today, I want to help you! I want you to be able to do everything you want in retirement. For the millennials who say YOLO –

you only live once, I agree with Joe Jordan, it's not YOLO. It's YOYO – YOU'RE ON YOUR OWN! The only person that will take care of your older self is your younger self. Be good to your future self! Let's get started...

"I Help People Become Millionaires"

ack in the late 80's and early 90's, when I was a MetLife agent, people would ask me, *"So what do you do?"* Does that ever happen to you? You know, you'll be at your kid's ball game, a party, or the golf course. You'll be somewhere in your church or wherever, and people will ask you what you do. What do you say?

Some people say, *"I'm a life insurance agent"* or *"I'm a financial advisor."* But do you know what I would say? *"I help people become millionaires. You tell me how many million you want, and I'll show you what you need to do to get there."*

That's got a little more pop to it, right?

Now, everybody's got their own little elevator speech but let me tell you what this did for me psychologically: it put me on the client's side (instead of me trying to sell them financial products).

Female (25) Millionaire, Female Age 25, Preferred Plus NT

Plan of Insurance	Whole Life 99
Base Face Amount	$500,000
Death Benefit - Year 1	$513,713
Dividend Option	Paid Up Additions (D)
Riders	Accelerated Benefit (EABR); PUA Rider, (Sched.); Index Participation

Policy Year	Age	Net After Tax Outlay	Cumulative Net After Tax Outlay	Net Cash Value	Increase in Net Cash Value	Net Death Benefit
1	25	7,715	7,715	2,730	2,730	513,713
2	26	7,715	15,430	5,769	3,039	527,063
3	27	7,715	23,145	10,246	4,477	541,026
4	28	7,715	30,860	17,313	7,067	554,933
5	29	7,715	38,575	24,472	7,159	568,286
6	30	7,715	46,290	32,766	8,296	581,569
7	31	7,715	54,005	41,325	8,557	596,795
8	32	7,715	61,720	50,376	9,051	611,983
9	33	7,715	69,435	59,528	9,152	627,416
10	34	7,715	77,150	69,094	9,567	642,206
11	35	7,715	84,865	79,787	10,693	657,985
12	36	7,715	92,580	91,266	11,479	676,310
13	37	7,715	100,295	102,133	10,867	694,683
14	38	7,715	108,010	115,716	13,585	712,721
15	39	7,715	115,725	130,243	14,525	736,959
16	40	7,715	123,440	145,764	15,521	762,602
17	41	7,715	131,155	162,335	16,571	789,602
18	42	7,715	138,870	180,032	17,696	817,986
19	43	7,715	146,585	198,906	18,874	847,737
20	44	7,715	154,300	218,835	19,929	878,658
36	60	7,715	277,740	727,724	46,194	1,521,359
37	61	7,715	285,455	776,496	48,771	1,574,028
38	62	7,715	293,170	827,955	51,460	1,628,753
39	63	7,715	300,885	882,303	54,347	1,685,673
40	64	7,715	306,600	928,639	57,336	1,744,920
41	65	7,715	316,315	1,000,162	60,523	1,806,636
42	66	0	316,315	1,056,195	56,033	1,857,819
43	67	0	316,315	1,115,301	59,107	1,911,632
44	68	0	316,315	1,177,616	62,315	1,968,140
45	69	0	316,315	1,243,337	65,720	2,027,465

Disclaimer: Please note that these numbers are based on a hypothetical example for illustrative purposes only.

As soon as I say that I'm now on their side. I'm part of their team—an active partner who is trying to help them become a millionaire.

Then I would run a life insurance illustration showing them what they'd have to do to have a million dollars by age sixty-five (or whatever age they were shooting for). Remember, back in the 80's, there were no illustrations of stock performance, mutual funds, etc. But life insurance policies all had illustrations.

For example, I would show a twenty-five-year-old female she would have to put $7,715 a year into this policy (table 1) to become a millionaire at her age 65.

Now we all know people shouldn't put all their money into a life insurance policy. We also know that there probably aren't a lot of twenty-five-year-olds that can afford to put $7,715 per year into their life insurance policy. So, then I would go to a time value of money calculator (table 2).

I would say, *"Well look at the following boxes one at a time. If you can get a 6 percent return, which I think is very doable over the long-term, you would have to put about $500 a month away. If you could get 9 percent (center box), you'd only have to put a little over $200 a month away. And if you could get 12 percent (bottom box), you'd only have to put $100 a month away."*

TABLE 2

Number of Periods (N)	40
Starting Amount (PV)	$ 0
Interest Rate (I/Y)	6%
Periodic Deposit (PMT)	$ 6,100

PMT made at the ● Beginning ○ End of each compound period

Calculate ●

Results

Future Value: $1,000,690.87

Number of Periods (N)	40
Starting Amount (PV)	$ 0
Interest Rate (I/Y)	9%
Periodic Deposit (PMT)	$ 2,750

PMT made at the ● Beginning ○ End of each compound period

Calculate ●

Results

Future Value: $1,012,802.63

Number of Periods (N)	40
Starting Amount (PV)	$ 0
Interest Rate (I/Y)	12%
Periodic Deposit (PMT)	$ 1,200

PMT made at the ● Beginning ○ End of each compound period

Calculate ●

Results

Future Value: $1,030,970.87

Disclaimer: Please note that these numbers are based on a hypothetical example for illustrative purposes only.

You may know higher interest rates result in either lower amounts of savings or higher amounts of accumulation. That's as intuitive as counting by fives or saying the ABCs. But here's the deal: many people don't understand this. These are just simple things I would explain to my clients on how to become wealthy.

I would sit with a client who would say "I don't want any risk. I'm just going to put my money into a CD. Well, if that CD is only paying 1%, it will take 72 years for you to double your money. But if you could get 10% per year, it only takes 7.2 years. That is a huge difference in wealth building capability.

I would explain backwards as well, that if they can earn a higher rate of return, they don't have to put as much away. I would tell them, *"If you have a lower rate of return, you have to put more away."* I mean, that's a simple concept, but I'm telling you most people really don't understand this.

CHAPTER 2

The 3 Phases of Wealth

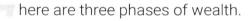here are three phases of wealth.

1. There's **building** wealth. (Who wants to be a millionaire?)

2. There's **protecting** wealth. (Who wants to stay a millionaire?)

3. And there's **distributing** wealth. (Who wants to live and give like a millionaire?)

I've spent my entire career focused on number two and number three. I teach people how to protect their wealth. Then I teach people how to distribute their wealth.

But what I'm going to do in this book is focus on number one: building wealth. I'm going to teach you the exact steps to becoming a millionaire. If you live in North America, you can absolutely become a millionaire. This book will show you how. These are the same techniques I have personally used and shared with my own children and grandchildren.

The 3 Keys to Building Wealth

There are really three keys to building wealth.

Number one, you want to make more money.

Number two, you want to spend less money. (That sounds very counterintuitive to most people, but you can't go on crazy, lavish spending sprees if you want to become a millionaire. You need to be very disciplined with your spending.)

Number three, you want to invest your money into appreciating assets. (Most people don't realize cars, boats, jet-skis, RVs, computers, iPhones, etc. are all depreciating assets. They go down in value every single day. Again, sounds simple, but many people simply don't think about it that way).

We'll All Earn Millions

I don't know who you are—and there will be many people reading this book—but I know for a fact you will earn millions of dollars over the course of your career. Just check out the following graphic (table 3).

- Lifetime earnings assuming a 40-year career with 3% annual increases

Initial Income	Lifetime Earnings	50-Year Career
$50,000	$3,770,062	$5,639,843
$100,000	$7,540,125	$11,279,686
$250,000	$18,850,314	$28,199,216

- The real question is, "How much will you KEEP?"

Disclaimer: Please note that these numbers are based on a hypothetical example for illustrative purposes only.

If you're making $50,000 a year over a forty-year career with 3 percent increases, you're going to make $3.7 million. If you work for fifty years, let's say from twenty to seventy, you're going to have $5.6 million. And if you can get to $100,000 of annual income, you're going to earn $7.5 million to $11.2 million. If I could get you to $250,000 a year of annual income, you're looking to make over $18.8 million over a normal forty-year career, and over $28 million over a fifty-year career.

So, the question isn't whether you're going to make millions. The real question is how much of that are you going to keep? Unfortunately, most people don't keep enough.

Back when I was an advisor, I would go to a person's house and show them life insurance, mutual funds, and investments, and they'd often say, *"I can't afford it."* Yet, I'd look around and see a satellite dish on the roof, two brand-new vehicles in the garage, an RV in the driveway, a jet ski by the dock, and enough technology to power a remote village. So it wasn't that they couldn't afford it. It was simply that they were making the wrong choices. They were spending on the wrong things. They were investing their money into DEPRECIATING assets.

Unfortunately, I realized that many people are standing at the back of the line. It was my job to move them to the front of the line by teaching them sound principles like paying yourself first, saving, investing, cutting spending, and being smart with investments.

The point is we're all going to make money, but if I can show you how to make more money, you can become wealthy faster. Again, you might think that's very simple, but I'm telling you many people don't even know how to think about this stuff.

So How Can You Make More Money?

I love the Japanese philosophy of *ikigai*, which is visually represented by four overlapping circles. I recommend everyone go through the exercise of writing down the answers to each of the items in these circles.

1. Begin by writing down things you're good at doing. These are the things you're known for being good at.

2. The second circle asks you to write down the things you *love* to do. Some people are good at stuff, but they hate doing it. That's not a great combo.

3. Third, what are the things the world needs?

4. And fourth, what can you get paid to do?

When you find the intersection of those four circles, that's *ikigai*. And I'm telling you, everything changed for me when I found my *ikigai*.

Everything changed for Jeremiah when he found his *ikigai*.

Likewise, everything will change for you when you find your *ikigai*. And one of the benefits will be you will likely make a whole lot more money.

Tom's Secret to Success

I would also like to share this secret of success with you. I've done it with my entire family—and here it is: *When you get a job, go to work early, stay late, and always do more than what you're paid to do.* Because soon you're going to become the most valuable worker in that company. You're going to get promoted faster. You're going to get paid more than all the other workers who come to work late, try to leave early, and do as little as possible for a paycheck.

Now again, this might seem obvious. When I was a kid, we were all trained on this, but I don't think kids today are trained in this. I can't tell you how many times people have used this concept and come back to me and said, *"Wow! This works!"*

For example, I remember when my second son, Sean, who is now an engineer in the Phoenix, Arizona area, turned seventeen years old. He applied for a position at a tennis resort in Fountain Hills, to be a locker room attendant.

I'll never forget, he came to me and said, *"Dad, there's no way I'm going to get hired. There are all these other people applying that are in their twenties and thirties, and they've been working for years. I have no experience. Nothing. I'm not going to get this job."*

I gave him the same advice I gave all my clients. I said, *"Sean, you go in there on that interview, and you tell them your dad is a retired lieutenant colonel. He's been tough on you your entire life. And he taught you that the secret to success is that you're going to come to work early, you're going to stay late, and you're always going to do more than what you're paid to do."*

And guess what? After he used those words on the interview, the guy closed his book, hired him on the spot, and canceled all the other interviews.

I am telling you this works. The people who implement this are the ones who get promoted and make more money. And that's the whole point. You want to be good at what you do. You want to make more money.

Abraham Lincoln said whatever you are, be a good one. If you're a plumber, be the best plumber in town. If you're a truck driver, be the best truck driver in your company. If you're a financial professional, qualify for MDRT (or whatever it is in your niche).

When I was in the Army, I'd gather my soldiers around and say, *"Guys, it's fun to be good. It is fun to be good because it's no fun to be bad."* I don't know if you've ever been bad at something, but that's no fun. People don't like you when you're bad. They're frustrated with you. It's no fun to be bad. It's fun to be good. So, get good at whatever you do. Whatever you are, be a good one.

There Are Riches in Niches

There are riches in niches. Find your niche, and it will make you rich. In many businesses too many of us are generalists. I was too. (I'm guilty, okay!) We try to do everything.

When I was brand new in the business, I was working for MetLife. If somebody could spell MetLife and write out a check, I was there. I'd drive across town to pick up a money market fund. It paid me zero commission. But if they were breathing and they could sign a check, I was there. I wanted the business.

But here's my advice to you: once you've established yourself a little bit, you need to find an area of expertise. Try to become an expert in a specific area. A Brain Surgeon is paid more than a General Practice Doctor. Whatever it is, you must find your niche.

My niche is retirement income. And within retirement income, there are various products and tools that can manage the risks in retirement. See, many people think retirement is about having some big pile of money. While that can certainly be helpful, retirement is about having increasing income and managing the many risks in retirement. That's my thing. That is what I do. I show people how to retire the optimal way – based on math and science, not some broker's opinion.

If I said it once, I'll say it a dozen times: there are riches in niches—so find your niche. It will make you rich.

Opportunity Cost

People don't miss out on becoming millionaires because they don't make enough money. It's because they spend too much of the money they make.

I believe most Americans could become millionaires except for two simple things. Number one, they spend way too much money on their cars. And number two, they get divorced.

The moral of the story is to drive a used car and stick with your first spouse. That sounds sort of tongue-in-cheek, but I'm serious.

Most Americans could become millionaires except for two things:

They spend WAY too much on cars.

They get divorced.

Moral of the story: drive a used car and stick with your first spouse!

To illustrate this, I'm going to show you how cars are keeping most people from becoming millionaires. And what better way to do this than by showing you an actual purchase decision I was personally working through recently.

Last year, I had the chance to buy a nice new Ford F-150 Lariat or Platinum. And when I was presented with the opportunity, I immediately began crunching the numbers. (That's what I do!)

In this situation, I could have bought a new F-150 for $65,000. But I also knew I could buy a 2-year-old Ford F-150 pickup with 13,000 miles for $30,000. Still a beautiful truck, but just a couple of years old with several thousand miles on it.

So, what did I do? Well, you can probably guess I went with the used model, which was $35,000 cheaper.

Why did I do that? Because I know if I take that $35,000, I would've spent on that brand new truck and I invest that, it's going to make me some serious money over the years. If I get 6 percent interest annually over thirty years, it grows to $210,000. In forty years, that's $383,000. And in fifty years, it balloons to $697,000. But that's just 6 percent. History says I'm likely to do a lot better than that.

If I could get 8 percent, it'd be $382,750 in thirty years, $849,588 in forty years, and $1,885,736 in fifty years. Now if I could get 10 percent, 12 percent, or 14 percent, of course I could do even better. But my point is this is just one vehicle!

I'm married with four kids. I don't know how many cars we've had over the years, but I would guess fourteen or fifteen of them. If I can buy a used car and make an extra $300,000 to $800,000 per vehicle over my lifetime . . . well, I'm going to be a lot more successful than my neighbor who's buying a brand-new car and trading it in every two years for another brand-new car. Many people today have car payments over $1,000 per month. They will likely never become millionaires doing that. That's not a recipe for becoming wealthy.

When I was a financial advisor in the Phoenix area, I typically drove red convertibles. I would buy a nice used one, drive it for 2 or 3 years and then would sell it. Often for the same or more than what I originally paid! The key was getting it for a great price and then selling it for a fair price. I went probably 10 years or more with literally no cost for my vehicle except for gas and maintenance. So, I know this is possible and can really help in wealth building.

I use cars as the example because everyone can associate with a big-ticket item like this, but it's not just a car thing. When you buy that handbag for $500, that's not a $500 handbag. That probably costs you $10,000 to $15,000 in retirement. That $30,000 boat can cost hundreds of thousands of lost retirement dollars.

Now I'm not saying don't have nice things. I've always driven nice vehicles. We've always gone on nice vacations. I even had a boat (but got a great price on a used one)! But what I'm trying to show you is when you're spending money today, it's not just the money you're spending today. It's what that money could have grown to if you didn't spend that money. That is called Opportunity Cost.

And what if I asked you in thirty years "Hey, what car did you drive twenty-seven years ago?" Number one, you wouldn't even remember. Number two, you wouldn't care if it was brand new or two years old.

My point is cars are the one thing that have the potential to really move the needle on your wealth. It's one of the most expensive repeat purchases people buy.

Digital marketing savant Gary Vaynerchuk once said, "People lose because they want things fast. But Life is Long" I love that quote. Life is long. You can't always get everything you want right now. It's easy to convince yourself you deserve it—especially in a credit-first culture—but just wait until you can pay cash for it. Just have some patience.

We live in a world where people love to say, "YOLO!" And yes, *you only live once* . . . but it's a long life. As my buddy Joe Jordan says, "It's not YOLO; it's YO-YO—*you're on your own*." The only one that's going to take care of your older self is your younger self.

These are the smart concepts I've shared with my clients over the years.

I'm trying to help you become wealthy. I want you to become a millionaire.

It's not going to be easy. (It's very simple, but it's not going to be easy.) I want you to be there, but you've got to understand this life is long. The government's not going to bail you out of this one.

CHAPTER 3

Financial Wellness Defined

inancial wellness really has to do with your relationship with money. Can you be financially independent and secure no matter what goes on? No matter if the market crashes; no matter if interest rates stay low; no matter if we see inflation . . . no matter, no matter, no matter? I'm going to be wealthy no matter any of those things because I've put protection into place. And this is where step two comes into play.

You are going to have to increase your financial knowledge. For years, I assumed people know certain things, but I learned that's a dangerous assumption. Most likely, nobody's gone over these concepts with most people. I would teach them how to do the following:

- **Increase their financial knowledge** so that they understand basic terminology and concepts as it relates to earning, spending, saving, investing, etcetera.

- **Change their attitude and behaviors on spending versus saving** so that they aren't spending every last penny on "nice" things that they *must have*.

- **Establish a habit of saving money.** Create smart behaviors so that these decisions become a regular rhythm in their lives.

- **Create behaviors that include money and financial planning.** It's about looking ahead, not just at the present day.

- **Be confident in achieving realistic financial goals.** For example, somebody making $18,000 per year isn't going to accumulate $1 million in retirement savings this year. Most people need to set a goal of $100,000 first, then $500,000, then $1 million, and so on. If it's not realistic, it's not going to work. Not everybody can jump right into that million-dollar level.

Obstacles to Financial Wellness

It's not all smooth sailing. There are plenty of obstacles to becoming financially independent and financially wealthy. Some of these hurdles are:

- **Not having a plan.** People don't plan to fail. They fail to plan. That was true thirty-five years ago, and it's still true today. Find a trustworthy advisor to sit down and work out a plan with you, that is the first step.

- **Having too much debt.** Most people are spending more than they earn. That is a recipe for financial disaster. Those people will never become wealthy.

- **No/Insufficient emergency fund.** Most people I've worked with in the past didn't have an emergency fund when they came to me. They didn't have any funds set aside for unplanned expenses.

If your car breaks down, you don't want to have to take money out of your 401(k). Or if your kid gets sick, you don't want to have to cancel your whole retirement plan. You need to have an emergency fund of at least three months. (And after this pandemic experience, I think twelve months to 2 years should be the new standard.)

- **Divorce.** I can't tell you how important it is to teach your children that picking their life partner is the most important decision they're going to make.

The best illustration of this is a successful friend of mine, whom we'll call Jerry. When Jerry was in his forties, he had millions of dollars. Then over the next twelve years, he had three divorces. His $2 million shrunk to $1 million. Then it went down to $500,000.

...getting divorced is a devastating financial event – to both partners.

Then it shrunk to $250,000. He is now trying to find places in Guatemala or Nicaragua to retire because he can't live here.

Now to be clear, I'm not saying to stay in an abusive relationship. I'm simply saying that getting divorced is a devastating financial event – to both partners.

- **Not maintaining a good credit rating.** This can cause all your different interest rates to be higher, which basically robs you of cash today (which could be working for you).

Having a Plan Helps You Figure Out:

- **What are your priorities?** Couples need to agree on priorities. In most households, there's a spender and a saver. Know which one you are and work together to agree on your priorities. It's almost impossible to become a millionaire if you don't agree on the big things.

- **What are you saving for?** Retirement, college, first house? Make sure everyone is on the same page regarding both short-term and long-term savings goals.

- **How much can you (or should you) save?** You *should* get to a point where you're saving at least 15 percent to 20 percent of your income. That may not be realistic at first, but you want to get to that point. Increase your savings with every pay increase. Avoid lifestyle creep!

- **When will you need this money?** Always be looking at the time horizon for your money. You'll need some money in three years, other money in ten years, and then you won't need to touch some money for twenty-five or thirty years. There are different ways to leverage funds based on when the money will be needed.

- **What changes do you need to make to accomplish this?** Recognizing issues and inhibiting factors sooner rather than later is a key to financial success.

- **How will you measure success/failure?** Figure out what success looks like for you. It could be a dollar amount, a certain lifestyle, an investment strategy, or something else. What does it look like for you? And how will you measure it to know if you're tracking?

- **Should you work with a financial professional?** My recommendation is an absolute YES! Look, I know this stuff inside and out, and I still use a financial advisor. Why? Because I don't keep up to date with the latest products, features, payout rates, etcetera. There are thousands of products out there. I need someone to help me find the exact right products for me! You should want that too.

CHAPTER 4

Saving and Investing for Retirement

Retirement Can Seem
a Long Way Off...

*I*t's helpful to view retirement like this image of a young lady staring at a mountain. Because when you're in your twenties and thirties, retirement seems so far away.

It's easy to say, *"Well, I'll worry about that when I'm fifty."* But the only problem is fifty comes faster than you know. And if the money's not there, it's not there.

The one thing young people have is time. Time is one of the most important ways of becoming wealthy. You're not going to become wealthy overnight. People are putting their money in Dogecoin or Reddit stocks like AMC and GME. And look, I'm not against that—but that's speculation. That's not investing. That is speculation.

I put 1 percent of my portfolio into speculation. I see too many people putting all their money into speculation, and that is not how you're going to become wealthy. That's how you're going to become dead broke.

Roadblocks to a Wealthy and Comfortable Retirement

Building long-term wealth doesn't just happen. Whether you're ten months, ten years, or forty years away from retiring, there are some considerations to consider. You must avoid the most common roadblocks to a wealthy and comfortable retirement.

1. Failure to Plan

ROADBLOCK #1: FAILURE TO PLAN

WORKERS

Only 42% of workers have tried to determine a retirement savings target

58% have no idea how much they will need in retirement

Know How Much They Need   Don't Know How Much They Need

Source: Copeland, Craig, et al. 2017 RCS: Many Americans Are Stressed About Retirement, Aren't Taking Steps to Prepare. Employee Benefit Research Institute, 2017. https://www.ebri.org/docs/default-source/ebri-pressrelease/pr4bb84f9d443d6688bc58ff0000a8d73a.pdf?sfvrsn=fd85292f_0

Only 42 percent of workers have ever even tried to determine how much they need to save for retirement. An astonishing 58 percent of people have no idea how much they're going to need.

More than 42 percent of workers between the ages of eighteen to twenty-nine have no retirement savings. And 26 percent of workers aged thirty to forty-four have no retirement savings. Shockingly, 17 percent of workers aged forty-five to fifty-nine have no retirement savings.

What are these people going to do?

2. Cost of Living

ROADBLOCK #2: COST OF LIVING

Effect of 3% inflation on purchasing power

Today	in 10 years	in 20 years
$40,107	$53,900	$72,400

"Source: Average New-Vehicle Prices Up 2% Year-Over-Year in July 2020, According to Kelley Blue Book" Kelley Blue Book, 2020. https://mediaroom.kbb.com/2020-08-03-Average-New-Vehicle-Prices-Up-2-Year-Over-Year-in-July-2020-According-to-Kelley-Blue-Book

Inflation is the next roadblock. While it's been "dead" for the last thirty years, it's suddenly back on the radar screen. And to be honest, I don't care if we are ever in a deflationary environment—inflation is always a factor. There are always going to be pockets of inflation.

The way I see it, I don't think healthcare costs are going down anytime soon. I don't think wages are going down. I don't think college costs are going down anytime soon, either. I don't think many things are going down.

This graphic shows that if we just have 3 percent inflation, that $40,000 car today is going to cost almost $54,000 in ten years.

In twenty years, it'll cost you $72,000. And that's just cars. Everything else is going up as well.

3. Burden of Taxes

Third, I believe taxes are going to be much higher in the future! In this chart, you can see the history of the U.S. marginal tax rate. For most of your parents' lives, it was over 70 percent. After World War II, it was over 90% for a few years! Now, we're somewhere in the 30 percent to 40 percent range.

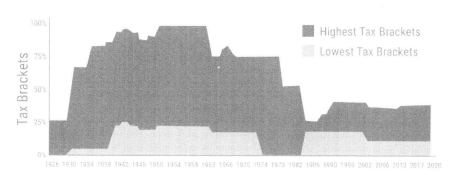

ROADBLOCK #3: HIGHER FUTURE TAXES

Tax rates are currently at historically low levels, suggesting they may be higher when you retire.

The graph above illustrates the high and low marginal federal income tax rates over history. Exemptions, deductions and state and local taxes are not taken into account when illustrating the marginal tax rates. Your actual tax rates may vary from those shown on the graph. Remember that historical rates are not a guarantee of future rates).

Source: "How Have the Top and Bottom Tax Brackets Changed Over Time?" National Taxpayers Union Foundation, 2021. https://www.ntu.org/foundation/tax-page/how-have-the-top-and-bottom-income-tax-brackets-changed-over-time

Having said all of that, you want to get on a track where you can have tax-free income as well. That's where cash value life insurance fits. That's where Roth IRAs and Roth 401(k)s fit. And you can fund Roth IRAs and 401(k)s with income annuities to have tax-free income for the rest of your life . . . guaranteed.

I have personally converted almost all of my IRAs and 401(k)s to Roth IRAs. Most of them are in income annuities. Additionally, I have moved more of my personal wealth to cash value life insurance. Those policies will give me even more tax-free income for life. I believe that setting yourself up for increasing tax-free income will be one of the most important things you can do for your retirement!

4. Procrastination

THE HIGH COST OF WAITING

$100 per month invested at 6%

- Donna waits 10 years
- Tom starts immediately

(Chart showing values: 10 Years — $0, $16,388; 20 Years — $16,388, $46,204; 30 Years — $46,204, $100,452)

This hypothetical example of mathematical compounding is used for illustrative purposes only and does not represent any specific type of investment. It does not include the impact of expenses, fees, or taxes, which would have reduced the results of the illustration. Actual results will vary.

Next comes procrastination. My whole career, I've heard people say things like, *"Yeah, Tom, that's good, but you know what? I'll just wait to do it next year. You know, we've got some things going right now. I'll start next year. We're just twenty-five. Come on, we've got time."*

Well, okay – but be very careful!

Just check out this graphic. Tom started investing immediately. Donna waited ten years. After ten years of making $100 monthly contributions at a 6 percent annual return, Tom has $16,388. After ten years, Donna has nothing.

In twenty years, Tom has $46,204. Donna has $16,388.

In thirty years, Tom has over $100,000. Donna? She's got just $46,204.

This just goes to show you how time makes all the difference in the world. If you're young, the best thing you have going for you is time. The worst retirement decision you can make is to waste this time advantage. The best time to start saving for retirement was yesterday. The second-best time is today...

5. Competing Priorities

Competing priorities are a very real threat. People will say, *"I've got to save for this down payment on a house. I have to put my kid through school. We must save for college. And now you want me to save for retirement?"*

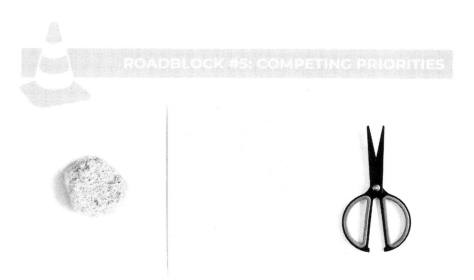

Hey, I get it! I've got 4 kids and 3 grandkids. I know all about competing priorities. We want to put them through college, my wife wants to go on a nice vacation, and our air conditioner went out unexpectedly. Yes, we all have to deal with this, but that's what you have to do. You have to understand there will always be competing priorities, but retirement can't be your last priority.

6. Lack of Financial Knowledge

Finally, there's a general lack of financial knowledge.

If you haven't already seen it yourself, let me be the first to tell you:

- Many people don't really know what a mutual fund is.
- They don't know what an ETF is.
- They don't know what bonds are.
- They don't know they can lose money in government bonds.

- They don't know the Rule of 72.
- They don't understand how interest on debt works.

They don't know.

The average person doesn't know a lot of stuff (when it comes to money). That's not a knock on their intelligence—just a byproduct of a system that doesn't teach financial literacy.

CHAPTER 5

A Few Words about Debt

ook, I'm not Dave Ramsey when it comes to debt. Dave basically says all debt is bad. That just isn't true. I'm not a big fan of debt, and I am personally debt free. However, I have used debt wisely in the past. Buying a home with a mortgage is not bad debt. A home is an APPRECIATING asset. It goes up over time. So, buying a home over 30 years is not a bad thing. I do have to say that people don't understand how mortgages work.

Vlad Meltzer is a Financial Professional who specializes in Debt Elimination. He says many people believe that a mortgage is the cheapest money you can borrow. That is not true. The way banks amortize the interest means most of your initial payments will be interest. Even if someone thinks they have a 3% mortgage, 59% of the first month's payment is interest.

For a 7% mortgage it's 87%. Even after 10 years, 47% of the payments are interest on the 3% mortgage and 75% on the

7% mortgage. Over 30 years, a 3% mortgage on a $200,000 home would cost $303,556.14. So, the $103,556.14 of interest is 51.8% of the $200,000 (This is the Total Interest Percentage (TIP)).

Vlad represents debt elimination cash flow management GPS which helps people and organizations to eliminate debt within 5-10 years without refinancing, debt consolidation, or budget cuts.

> *...borrowing money can give you leverage. You are using someone else's money to make money.*

I don't want to get deep in the weeds but there are some interesting Home Equity Lines of Credit and other ways to pay the home off faster because the loan is amortized differently. Australia, for example, has a totally different way of handling home loans. My point is that borrowing money can give you leverage. You are using someone else's money to make money.

But leverage can cut both ways. Buying "stuff" with credit cards is not good debt. You are paying interest to buy DEPRECIATING assets (cars, boats, jet skis, RV's, furniture, clothes, etc.). You want to limit and eliminate, if possible, using credit to buy things that go down in value.

Now we all need some things, but many of us are putting way too much money into depreciating assets. Borrowing money to do this is doubly bad!

Some people say that student loans are good debt. I'm skeptical. Student loan debt in American now exceeds credit card debt! Giving large sums of money to 18-year-olds at college doesn't seem very wise to me. Too much of that money finds a way to buy pizza, beer, and wild spring breaks!

I told my kids I would not pay for all their college. I wanted them to contribute. I did make sure that NONE of them had any student loan debt when they graduated. I see way too many 25-year-olds with $50,000, $100,000, or more of student debt. Now if you are a doctor or lawyer, maybe it made sense. But if you are a barista at Starbucks because you majored in German Poetry, maybe it wasn't a good decision...

People say that business loans are good debt. Well, they certainly can be. I lent my oldest son some money when he was building his first business. He paid me back in full and now owns many businesses. That was a very good use of debt.

On the other hand, about 70-80% of businesses fail in their first 5 years. The debt they took on doesn't go away. So now they have a failed business PLUS a bunch of debt that they will be paying off for years.

So, in general, if you use debt wisely to purchase appreciating assets, debt can be a great tool. But if you use debt to finance risky ventures (stock margin debt) or for depreciating assets, I strongly encourage you to think twice.

I'm often asked if someone should pay off their house early. The answer? It depends. If you have a 2% mortgage but can buy a government bond paying 5%, at least financially, it doesn't make sense to pay off your house early. I say "financially" because there may be other reasons why you want to pay off the house.

I'm one of those people who doesn't like to be in debt. I own my homes free and clear; I buy my cars with cash. That may not technically be the smartest thing to do financially but for my peace of mind, it makes complete sense. So, I will leave that decision to you.

CHAPTER 6

Advisors who "Get it."

A long time ago, I learned my job was to educate people financially. Let me share a few examples of advisors around the country who are doing the same for their clients.

Jeff Tamas, RICP™

Jeff Tamas, RICPTM is the CEO of Ideal Retirement Solutions in Southwest Florida. He is a financial advisor who both helps his clients become wealthy but then also helps them protect that wealth and ultimately distribute that wealth to themselves with investments and guaranteed lifetime income. He also works with them to help their families using life insurance and other estate planning tools. He has been a diligent student of mine through the years.

Jeff says, "As I think back over the years and replay the countless meetings I've had with clients that range from those who are just getting started to those who are at the proverbial retirement finish line, there are few things that stick out to me that you might find beneficial at your current stage."

Starting with retirement distribution, there are two main things he hears from people who are ready to retire:

- "I wish I started investing sooner."
- "I would do things differently if I had a second chance."

Whatever you do, make sure that this isn't you twenty, thirty, or even forty years from now.

"If you are just getting started on your retirement planning journey, you possess something extremely valuable that people who are in their latter stages will never have again: time! Don't let it slip away; leverage it every day to make sure you set yourself up for a secure financial future," Jeff says.

He continues: "I have to agree that time is just as important a factor as rates of return, what asset class you invest in, and how well diversified you are. I have stated in the past that it is the money you save in your twenties that will allow you to retire in your sixties!"

When I asked him for his biggest piece of advice for smart financial decision-making for younger clients, he said he likes to prepare and coach them about the future cost of spending money.

"For example, if they are a family of four and purchased Disney passes for the year. That will set them back right around $6,000," Jeff says. "I then educate my clients to view the expense through a different lens. I explain to them that if they invested that money at an 8 percent growth rate over the course of ten years, it would be equal to $13,320. I equip them to ask the big question: 'Is that Annual Disney pass worth $13,320?' In that situation, my position is to challenge their thought process and educate them to make the best choice for their family."

It's also a great idea to determine if you value experiences or possessions more. For Jeff and his wife Vanessa, they prefer experiences over things. So that's what they spend on.

"The last thing you ever want to do is deprive yourself of a quality of life now, every spending decision has to be made with wisdom," he says.

In Jeff's eyes, emotional spending and a lack of patience are often at the root of poor financial decision making. That's why he encourages people to wait seventy-two hours before making any significant choices.

Caleb Guilliams

 As the oldest of 6 kids in a homeschooled family, Caleb grew up in Central Wisconsin. Ever since he can remember, he has always been fascinated with how money worked.

At the age of 17, Caleb got a job at a community bank in his hometown. By 19 years old, he was one of the youngest to take over the bank's entire investment department, getting to see firsthand how most Americans were financially failing.

After three years of traveling the country and being mentored by some of the most successful financial minds, Caleb became passionate about helping people find a better way to build wealth. Leaving his prestigious position at the bank, Caleb founded BetterWealth at the age of 21, authored a best-selling book "The AND Asset" at age 22, began hosting the Better Wealth Podcast, and spoke to thousands around the world.

Caleb now lives in Nashville with his wife April and leads a virtual company with members all over the country. Caleb's mission is to, "Help people see and reach their highest potential," which is evident in the way he passionately talks to people about becoming wealthy. Caleb's philosophy "Wealth Equals Intentional Living." Breaking down intentional living into four major categories (time, relationships, skills, and resources), Caleb will go as far as to say, "You're not wealthy if you're not living intentionally."

From a financial perspective, Caleb would say cash flow is the most important metric. You might have a high net worth, a great credit score, or an amazing rate of return on your portfolio, but cash flow is what pays the bills and makes your intentional life a reality. Think of cash flow as the lifeblood of your intentional life. Caleb is also a huge fan of the word efficiency. Efficiency, Caleb would say, is the universal theme we should all want in our lives. He defines efficiency as, "Removing any friction that gets in the way of your desired result."

Caleb then walked me through his Five Part Wealth Framework on how BetterWealth helps their clients maximize wealth through the lens of efficiency.

Clarity

The first step is clarifying your definition of wealth (i.e. how would you define your intentional life?). One question Caleb likes to ask is, "If money wasn't an issue, what would you be doing and why would you be doing it?" This question helps get to the deeper heart issue and starts to help you gain clarity on what you truly want. ROR, for many, stands for Rate of Return. Since many people don't have clarity on what they truly want, they let the Rate of Return be the driving force of what they should do with their money.

However, Caleb's definition of ROR is "Return On Result," meaning we should be looking at our time, relationships, skills, and resources, which includes our finances, through the lens of results while using intentional living as the measuring metric. Action step: What is your intentional living metric? Audit your time, relationships, skills, and resources, and then see how they align with your intentional living metric. The next four steps will help with this audit.

Create Value

Step two is about understanding why cash flow is the most important financial metric and how it follows value creation. Cash flow is generated, in its simplest form, through value exchange. Understanding how this equation works will be key. Think of money as little IOUs for value. Value can be made up of a service or product, but these are really the only two categories of value. For example, service could be you working for someone else, or starting a business that provides a service to your clients.

The money that follows from the service is based on the perception of the value you provide. Most people divorce themselves from value creation when thinking long term, but a better goal is to have our financial resources produce continual value and generate enough cash flow on their own for us to live intentionally.

Some would call this retirement, some would call this financial freedom or passive income, but whatever your term is, when your financial resources create enough value for you to be able to live your life intentionally, you will have accomplished what many will sadly never experience. Action Step Value Audit – How am I providing value in the following areas: My time? My relationships? My skills? My resources?

Consumption

Once cash flow is created it can only do two fundamental things. It's either consumed, cash flow that is gone forever, or it's controlled, cash flow invested for the future to someday be consumed by you or a future generation. We call this fundamental principle the Cash Flow Ratio, representing how money can only do two things. When talking about consumption, I am talking about anything that pays for your current lifestyle. Your fixed and variable spending, food, gas, bills, rent, mortgage, debt service, taxes, etc.....

Think of consumption as the cost of doing life. The goal isn't to eliminate consumption because we all need to consume, but rather it's just being intentional with what and how we consume while being as efficient as possible with our consumption. When you lose a dollar to consumption you don't just lose the initial dollar, but what that dollar could do for you in the future because you will never be able to use that dollar again. This is called 'lost opportunity cost' and is by far the greatest wealth eroder you will experience.

Action Step: – Do you have a system for tracking your money? – Are you spending your money on what you value? – Do you know the difference between good debt and bad debt? If you have bad debt, do you know the best way to pay it off? – Are you overpaying on your taxes?

Step
4

Control Cash Flow

Cash Flow that isn't consumed is controlled. Caleb is a firm believer that your ability to control your cash flow will be key to living wealthy! The most profitable businesses in the world are those that control capital at scale. Banks are a good example of this.

All banks do is control money! They are institutions that get money to flow to them without friction, they limit their risk by making you provide the collateral with your home or car, they use leverage without massive risk, and they are masters at the velocity of cash flow.

Here are five lessons Caleb has learned about maximizing his control looking at banks:

Save More – Banks are masters at getting as much money to flow to them as possible. They will go as far as penalizing you for not having direct deposits because they care so much about systematic forced savings. How can you get more of your cash flow to flow to you?

Have Liquidity – Liquidity is the ability to access money. Banks have a massive amount of capital. Because banks have capital and fast access, they have endless opportunities. The takeaway: having liquidity for emergencies and/or opportunities, increases your control, not just from emergencies and the unknown, but also gives you an upside with future cash flow opportunities.

Reduce Risk – Banks are masters at reducing risk at all costs using underwriting and requiring the borrower to produce collateral protecting against the chance of loss. How can you reduce risk (limit your downside) in investing and utilizing your money?

Use Leverage – Banks create profit using leverage (i.e., other people's money) without taking on a crazy ton of risk. Leverage is anything that amplifies a result. What are ways we can leverage our dollars and give them more than one job without increasing risk?

Cash Flow Compounds – Banks see loans as assets. Receiving monthly cash flow payments from these loans makes them a valuable asset. How can we compound our assets to produce more cash flow?

Step 5

Cover Your Assets from Risk

The last part of the wealth framework is covering and protecting your assets from risk, starting with your greatest asset: yourself! Contrary to what many believe, Caleb believes anyone can become wealthy without taking unnecessary risks. The most direct definition of risk is "your exposure to danger". In wealth creation or wealth management, these dangers can come in all shapes and sizes. It's important to know that you can't shield yourself from every dangerous situation, but you can mitigate or manage the exposure these damages can cause to you and your current future cash flow. We call this risk management.

The use of insurance can be one of the most efficient ways to cover your assets and protection against risk.

Action Step: Of the following, are these areas efficiently protected from risk? If your answer is 'no' or 'unsure' Caleb highly encourages you to find a professional to help in that area. Loss of income due to market volatility? Loss of income due to death? Loss of income due to disability? Current and future health care? Home and auto insurance? Lawsuits?

Future taxation? Identity theft? I will also note that Caleb and his team are big fans of using max-funded life insurance to help their clients maximize wealth efficiency. He calls life insurance an "And Asset" because when set up and used properly it becomes a safe asset that gives multiple uses to your dollar and can enhance all five steps of the BetterWealth Framework.

CHAPTER 7

Where are YOU on the Mountain?

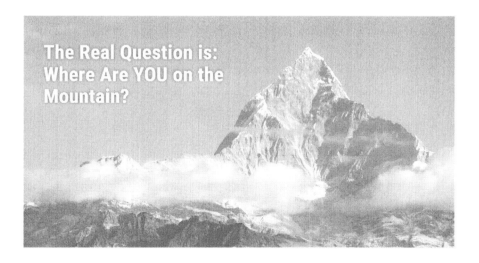

The Real Question is:
Where Are YOU on the
Mountain?

*L*et's go back to the mountain. There's building wealth, protecting wealth, and distributing wealth. The question is where are you on the mountain?

If you are in your 20's, 30's, or 40's, you're in the building wealth phase. And to protect wealth and distribute wealth later, you must first build wealth. So, this is the logical place to start.

When it comes to building wealth, most people use traditional products: stocks, bonds, mutual funds, ETFs, real estate, etcetera. I would always try to explain the difference of these types of investments as simply as possible.

The simplest way to put it is stocks are *ownership* and bonds are *loanership*. How so? Well, let's use Apple as an example.

When you own Apple stock, you are one of the owners of Apple and all the products they sell. You get a piece of all the profits they make. You're one of the owners.

If you own an Apple bond, however, you don't own any of Apple. You have lent them money, and they have agreed to pay you back with interest. Maybe they pay a 2 percent interest. You give them $100,000. They guarantee to pay you 2 percent a year. That's a bond. Stocks are ownership, while bonds are loanership.

Mutual Funds are simply portfolios of stocks and/or bonds that are managed by a professional money manager. The price of a mutual fund is set every day at the close of the stock market.

An ETF is like a mutual fund except you can buy or sell at any time during the day. You don't have to wait for the market to close to know your buy/sell price.

Both mutual funds and ETFs can invest in assets other than stocks and bonds, but, again, I am trying to keep things simple.

Real estate can be your home, a vacation home, rental property, commercial real estate, and REIT's (Real Estate Investment Trusts).

I don't get into detail with these products because there are many other books that do that.

Investment Challenges

The traditional 60/40 portfolio has struggled recently. In fact, 2022 was the worst year in decades for the 60/40 portfolio. Bond interest rates started low, but when the Fed raised interest rates so quickly, bonds tanked. 2022 was the worst year ever for bond returns. I wrote a newsletter in 2016—my second-most popular newsletter—all about how the 60/40 portfolio is no longer a best practice. It's dead. You can go read it for yourself, but I basically said that if younger people are normally in a 60 percent stock, 40 percent bond portfolio, they should switch that to 60 percent stock, 40 percent cash value life insurance.

Why? Because a life insurance policy, like whole life or IUL, is likely going to earn a bond-like return of 3 percent to 6 percent. But it doesn't have the interest rate risk bonds do right now.

If interest rates go up, the value of bonds goes down. People don't understand that, but they need to.

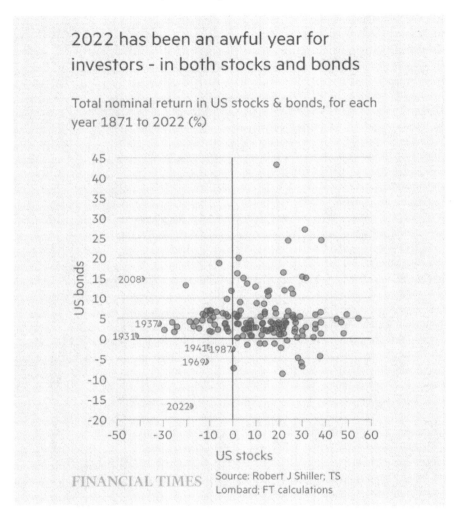

2022 has been an awful year for investors - in both stocks and bonds

Total nominal return in US stocks & bonds, for each year 1871 to 2022 (%)

FINANCIAL TIMES   Source: Robert J Shiller; TS Lombard; FT calculations

Many people "poo poo" the power of permanent life insurance as a wealth-building tool. However, people like Walt Disney and JC Penney realized the value of life insurance. In fact, those businesses would not have existed without those life insurance policies they used to start those businesses. Think of all the farmers and ranchers who dipped into their life insurance policies to provide the cash to run their farms during the bad years.

So many people misunderstand whole life and universal life. They think the premium is the cost of the policy. Nothing could be further from the truth.

With permanent life insurance policies, you actually want to put as much money as you can into the policies. Permanent life insurance is not an expense; it is an asset. Just to put it into perspective, my whole life premium is $226,000 per year. If you want a lot of tax-free income in retirement, you need to put a lot of money in.

What about people sixty and above? If they're 60 percent stock, 40 percent bond, I would recommend moving the bonds into an income annuity. Why? Because inside the portfolio, the income annuity functions like a AAA-rated bond with a CCC-rated yield with zero standard deviation. Ernst and Young just wrote a whitepaper trying to determine the very best mix for an investment portfolio.

They tried 100% stock, 90% stock/10% bond, 80/20. 70/30, 60/40, 50/50. Then they went back and added some cash value life insurance and an income annuity. Guess what they discovered? The best portfolio contained investments, cash value life insurance and income annuities. I have known this for over 30 years. It is great to see other investment professionals finally figuring it out!

At the end of 2021, stock valuations were at all-time record highs. Interest rates were near all-time record lows. In 2022, as discussed previously, we had a completely opposite situation. The future holds more volatility I'm afraid.

S&P 500®

January 2010 – December 2020

3669

2,584
3/31/20
Worst Q1
Ever

11-Year equity bull rally – Recent Market Volatility

10-Year U.S. Treasury Yield

January 2010 – December 2020

0.70%
3/31/20
0.95%

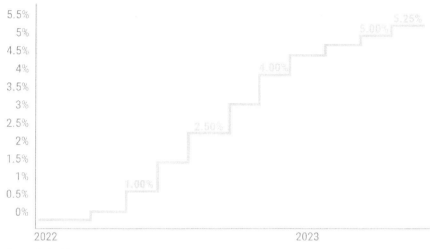

Source: Federal Reserve

CHART 2: S&P 500 PERFORMANCE FROM 4/30/2020 TO 6/30/2023

Source: Federal Reserve

The question becomes how much risk can retirees (or those close to retirement) really take? And I think too many of them have too much risk in their portfolio. Unfortunately, they don't take advantage of the buying opportunities when the market does crash (because markets do crash). And when they crash, that's unfortunately when most people sell. But it's really when they should be buying. You buy low and you sell high. But what do most people do? They buy high and they sell low.

CHAPTER 8

A Little More About Life Insurance

s I said earlier, life insurance is a very misunderstood asset class. Let's hear from a couple of entrepreneurs who "get it."

Dave Resseguie describes himself as the Chief Shepherd of The Resseguie Group (https://theresseguiegroup.com) based in South Florida. Dave's initial goal in life was to become a preacher. But he instead found himself in the insurance business—and he quickly became a successful advisor specializing in life insurance, along with disability and long-term care coverage.

He later transitioned his focus within both Northwestern Mutual and MassMutual taking on the role of training and development, where he oversaw the recruiting of agents for multiple offices and educating agents on how to grow their businesses and present coverage.

In 2011, Dave founded The Resseguie Group, which specializes in working with top insurance advisors—one-on-one and in groups—teaching habits and discipline that drive productivity and high retention. The company does so virtually and in person via one-time speaking engagements, as well as through ongoing strategic training partnerships.

On tips for making more money, Dave's best advice is to bet on yourself.

"Fear and limiting beliefs will tend to hold you back. Your faith needs to be greater than your fear," he says. "For me, one of the most critical elements of achieving this level of growth is to have clarity of focus. That clarity of focus has come through having an emotional vision of our future that we are deeply connected to."

Since 2011, Dave's team has seen their top line revenue grow at an average of over 25 percent per year.

As far as life insurance goes, Dave notes many consumers perceive term life coverage as being more expensive than it is—and they are happily surprised to learn just how much death benefit can be purchased for such a low premium amount.

While Dave believes in both term and permanent coverage, he describes whole life insurance as one of the last tax-efficient financial vehicles left for consumers to grow and protect wealth, as well as to access funds tax-free. "Permanent life insurance is a great warehouse for cash," he explains.

He also states whole life insurance policy holders shouldn't think of the premium as a "cost" but rather as a contribution to a program that has value—especially from a longer-term perspective.

He values whole life insurance so much he has policies on all three of his young children—not necessarily just for the death benefit but also for the cash value that can be used later in life to fund college costs, a wedding, or even a down payment on a first home.

...borrowing money can give you leverage. You are using someone else's money to make money.

Plus, getting into a permanent policy early in life can ensure a child's insurability and lock in a low premium for the remainder of their life. Unfortunately, Dave's family experienced the loss of one of his daughter's good friends at age two.

Most people purchase life insurance to provide for:

- Mortgage / debt payoff

- Funding children's school / activities / life events

- Ongoing, guaranteed, after-tax income.

Once people learn about all the things permanent life insurance can do, many of Dave's clients have told him they "didn't know life insurance worked this way."

Dave says permanent life insurance can be looked at like contributing into a 401(k) plan with a significant "matching" contribution where the funds in the account grow tax-deferred but can also be accessed tax-free (through a loan) like a Roth IRA—all this along with death benefit protection as well as locking in future insurability.

 David H. Kinder RFC®, ChFC, CLU is the owner of David Kinder Insurance and Financial Wealth Solutions. He is a nearly twenty-year veteran of the insurance and financial services industry. He has served the needs of residents and business owners in Southern California in a variety of capacities, currently as a financial consultant working with families, retirees, and business owners to use unconventional strategies to help them accomplish their retirement income and wealth accumulation goals.

He studied advanced financial planning through his various studies with The American College of Financial Services as well as being a student of other great minds in the insurance and financial services industry. What I love about David is his commitment to learning and then sharing that knowledge with others. He runs numerous insurance and investment groups on Facebook. He has put together a wealth of knowledge of written and video presentations he shares with his followers.

He encourages licensed financial professionals to join both of his Facebook groups called "Professional Life Agent Insurance Discussions" ("PLAID") at www.Facebook.com/groups/lifeinsurance and "Advanced Whole Life Insurance Agent Discussions" at www.Facebook.com/groups/wholelifeinsurance. The "PLAID" group is far larger (currently over 13,000 members) and we discuss almost everything related to the insurance and financial services business. In addition, he holds regular 'group expert' webinars with industry influencers, speakers, and leaders in their specializations so the entire group can benefit. The 'whole life' group is much smaller (currently just under 1,000 members) and is far more focused on specific strategies, companies, and product design. And yes, we discuss IUL and other policies as well.

***

David teaches people to not become a victim of the stock market by turning bad news into opportunities.

"I believe that the rules of personal financial planning have fundamentally changed since 2008," David says. "We all know what happened that year: leveraged mortgage derivative securities failed and sent the stock market into a free-fall, losing 50 percent of its value in two months! Until 2008, losses were generally far more bearable by comparison (if you'll pardon the pun!)."

"Where is it written in personal finance that to make money you must lose 30 percent, 50 percent, or even 70 percent of your money? There is a phrase that is common in the investment advisor world: 'Volatility is the price we pay for higher returns', but do you really see higher returns? Or is that just a phrase advisors say to help calm clients and investors during turbulent times?" These are the questions David now asks in a post-2008 world.

"Before 2008, I used to reference just a 10 percent loss as the downside of an investment. How much return would you need to get back to where you were the next year? Just an 11 percent return," David explains. "Now, in a post-2008 world, if you had a 50 percent loss, how much money would you need to get back to where you were the next year? One hundred percent! You would need a 100 percent gain the next year to get back to where you were. How likely is that to happen? For many mutual funds, they took about five years to get back to their pre-crash levels. Can your financial plan afford a five-year setback?"

David believes the adage of "buy and hold" is now completely outdated due to new understandings of economics following the Baby Boomer generation of spending patterns and new levels of uncertainty in our financial decisions.

David believes, "It would probably be more accurate to say, 'buy, hold, and pray' these days."

"How can we not be a victim of the stock market, gain control, and perhaps even take advantage of these events? I believe that by having a non-correlated reserve asset that you can tap into when you choose is one of the best ways to take advantage of stock market volatility," he explains.

How can this work?

Suppose you have cash values in a life insurance wealth contract immune to stock market volatility, David suggests. Today, that would be a whole life, or an indexed universal life insurance wealth contract structured primarily for cash value accumulation rather than death benefits. When the market declines, you have money (when many others are doing the "buy and hold" game). Declines create panic and more uncertainty, but according to David, you have cash and capital you can access.

"Borrow against your life insurance policy and invest in what you choose. Be sure to keep that investment for at least twelve months so you can be taxed at capital gains rates instead of ordinary income tax rates on the performance of the investment," David says. "After the investment grows and rebounds, sell off the investment and repay the loan. Keep the profits, minus the taxes to be paid. Rinse and repeat as many times as you wish. Turn bad news into your opportunities!"

Now, of course, this is not securities investment advice, David makes it clear. You'll want to do your homework on what you would prefer to invest in, such as Exchange Traded Funds (ETFs), mutual funds, individual stocks, bonds, or even a managed portfolio. But in his decades of experience, the best way to take charge of your investment decisions is through the proper leverage of a properly funded cash value life insurance policy.

"Does this need to be limited to stock market investments? No! If you are a business owner with capital, you can use this to buy inventory from suppliers that may go out of business," David mentions. "If you are a real estate investor, you can use this to buy more real estate—particularly foreclosed properties! There are many ways to benefit by having such a capital reserve because you have cash and capital when others don't."

Tom Chimes In

Let me add another reason for cash value life insurance – it is protected from creditors in many states. For example, I live in Arizona. All the money I put into annuities and life insurance is creditor protected. What does that mean? It means it CANNOT be taken from me by a lawsuit.

I have watched people work their entire lives saving and investing. As they are near or in retirement, something happens – an accident, a business transaction gone bad, an unhappy client or employee, a huge medical bill, and "poof," it's gone. They were sued and lost much of their wealth. I sure didn't want that to happen to us.

There are some exceptions. You can find those and the status of Creditor Protection in your state here: https://www.insuranceandestates.com/life-insurance-creditor-protection-by-state/

CHAPTER 9

Building Wealth

TABLE 5: HOW FAST CAN AN INVESTMENT GROW?

Hypothetical Illustration

The Rule of 72

- At a 10% return, money will double every 7.2 years

- To use this rule, simply divide the annual return into 72

Hypothetical Annual Return	Years to Double
72 / 12.00%	6
72 / 8.00%	9
72 / 4.00%	18
72 / 2.00%	36
72 / 1.00%	72

Securities have inherent risks, including fluctuating earnings, yield, and dividends. Investments are subject to adverse or unpredictable market conditions and other factors. The Rule of 72 is a hypothetical mathematical calculation and does not represent any specific type of investment. It does not include the impact of expenses or fees, which would have reduced the results of the illustration. There is no assurance that any investment will double within a specific timeframe.

Disclaimer: Please note that these numbers are based on a hypothetical example for illustrative purposes only.

When discussing wealth building, I love using the Rule of 72. In fact, I find it to be one of the most effective ways to show people their potential for growing their wealth. This formula is a simple way to figure out how fast money doubles. You just take whatever interest rate a person is earning and divide it by 72. That tells you how long it will take to double your money. For example, a 10 percent return divided into 72; tells you your money will double every 7.2 years (table 5).

When I was an advisor, I would do is use a specific example with a client. So, let's say I was meeting with a client and they had $50,000 in their 401(k). I would say something like:

> "Okay, now you want this $50,000 to go to $100,000. And then you want that $100,000 to go to $200,000. And the $200,000 to $400,000 to $800,000 and so on. Well, this is how long it's going to take." I would walk them through how their investments can grow in different scenarios based on their principle.

Now if I had someone who said they want to keep it in the bank so that it's safe and secure, I would run the calculation based on a 1 or 2 percent return. They can quickly see how difficult it will be to become wealthy at those low rates. You have got to find higher returns to allow your money to grow faster. The key to becoming wealthy is not just to work for money but to get your money to work for you!

Timing Is Everything…and Timing Is Random

6.38%	5.32%	15.96%	13.83%	7.47%	14.89%	36.17%	
						1927	1928
						1933	1935
						1936	1938
		1929				1942	1943
		1932			1944	1945	1950
		1934	1947		1949	1951	1954
		1939	1948		1952	1955	1958
		1940	1956		1964	1961	1963
		1946	1960		1965	1967	1975
		1953	1970		1971	1976	1980
		1962	1978		1972	1982	1983
		1969	1984	1926	1979	1985	1989
1930		1977	1987	1959	1986	1991	1995
1931	1941	1981	1992	1968	1988	1996	1997
1937	1957	1990	1994	1993	2006	1998	1999
1974	1966	2000	2005	2004	2010	2003	2009
2002	1973	2015	2007	2014	2012	2013	2020
2008	2001	2018	2011	2016	2017		
-20% or lower	-10% to -20%	0% to -10%	0% to 8%	8% to 12%	12% to 20%	20% or greater	

Past performance is no guarantee of future results. Source: Morningstar, 12/31/13. S&P 500 total returns for large-company stocks 1926 to 2020 S&P 500 Index is an unmanaged index that is widely regarded as the standard for measuring large-cap U.S. stock market performance. An investment cannot be made directly into an index.

Another thing most people don't realize is the stock market is positive about 73 percent of the time, while it's negative about 27 percent of the time (table 6). For all of the people that think the stock market is just a gamble and they'll lose all of their money, that's simply not true. It's only been down 20 percent or more in a year six times since 1924. Six times!

But look at how many times it's been up over 20 percent. It's seventeen times! You obviously can't guarantee a rate of return, but if you just study some basic numbers from the past, it's easy to show people that over time the stock market goes up. Younger people have time to weather the ups and downs of the market. They just need to stay disciplined in the down years of the market.

Once people get into their 50's however, they need to realize that markets can go down and stay down for a long period of time. While it doesn't happen often, it could! Just look at the Japanese stock market. It's been down for over thirty years. The European stock market has been down for over twenty years. Even in America, we experienced the "lost decade" from 1999 to 2009 – the market did nothing. Retirees cannot afford waiting 10, 20, or 30 years to recover.

Let me ask you a question, *"What would happen to your portfolio if this market went down and stayed down for thirty years? How would your retirement look then?"* My guess is it would not look good.

That's why we put guarantees into the mix. That's where variable annuities with guaranteed benefits or fixed index annuities work. You get some of the upside but don't have to sweat over the downside.

I personally love having equity exposure, but I don't like losing money. So, I don't put a lot of money in the naked stock market. I put guarantees on my money.

TABLE 7: PSYCHONOMICS – INVESTOR BEHAVIOR PLAYS A KEY ROLE IN ACTUAL RETURNS

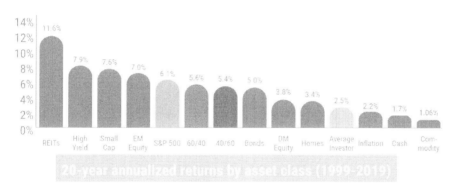

Source: Barclays, Bloomberg, FactSet, Standard & Poor's, J.P. Morgan Asset Management; (Bottom) Dalbar Inc., MSCI, NAREIT, Russell. Indices used are as follows: REITs: NARET Equity REIT Index, Small cap: Russell 2000, EM Equity: MSCI EM, DM Equity: MSCI EAFE, Commodity: Bloomberg Commodity Index, High Yield: Bloomberg Barclays Global HY Index, Bonds: Bloomberg Barclays U.S. Aggregate Index. Homes: median sale price of existing single-family homes, Cash: Bloomberg Barclays 1-3m Treasury, Inflation: CPI 60/40. A balanced portfolio with 60% invested in S&P 500 Index and 40% invested in high-quality U.S. fixed income, represented by the Bloomberg Barclays U.S. Aggregate Index. The portfolio is rebalanced annually. Average asset allocation investor return is based on an analysis by Dalbar Inc., which utilizes the net of aggregate mutual fund represent the 20-year period ending 12/31/19 to match Dalbar's most recent analysis. Guide to the Markets – U.S. Data are as of March 31, 2021.

Then there's psychonomics. This is all about investment behavior. We can say the stock market averages 12 percent a year since 1924 or that real estate investment trusts (REITs) have averaged 11.6 percent; however, the truth is the average investor has gotten just 2.5 percent (table 8).

How can that be? Well, it's because they don't buy low and sell high. They buy high and they sell low. They don't necessarily invest in Apple, Amazon, Google, and Facebook. They buy AMC, GME, and Dogecoin. Psychonomics is the reason why people aren't getting the rates of return they could (or should).

TABLE 8: THE CYCLE OF EMOTIONS: ECONOMICS VS. PSYCHONOMICS

The typical, emotional investor will buy something they're optimistic about, and they're excited. It keeps going up, which creates a thrill. The market tops off, and they think they're getting rich. They start thinking about how smart they are.

But then the market starts going down. Suddenly, they have anxiety. There might even be denial. *"It's just a temporary setback,"* they think. *"We'll be back on track. This is no big deal."*

Then there's fear. There's desperation. There's panic. There's capitulation. *"How could I be so stupid?"* There's despondency. There may even be some form of depression. And that is when people should buy. Because after this comes hope, relief, optimism, excitement, and thrill. The problem is people do the exact opposite.

I would communicate this entire life cycle to clients so that they can get a glimpse into the psychology behind it all.

What is fascinating in this is how health and finances are so closely related. In 2019, a Bankrate survey found more than half of Americans lose sleep over money troubles. High levels of financial stress are manifested through physical symptoms like sleep loss, anxiety, headaches, migraines, compromised immune system, digestive issues, high blood pressure, muscle tension, heart arrhythmia, depression, and feelings of being overwhelmed.

I know for a fact there are people reading this book who have lived through this. Why can I be so certain? Because I know I have.

I started out as a brand-new Second Lieutenant in the US Army back in 1983. At that time, a Second Lieutenant made $13,000 a year. Within two years, I had two little boys and a wife in Germany. Let me reiterate I was a married father of two stationed in Germany making $13,000 a year.

When I got out of the Army six years later, I was a captain making $36,000. In my first six years, I made very little money. I had two kids and a wife. We didn't have plates. We didn't have spoons. We didn't have blankets. We didn't have towels. We didn't have anything. We had to buy all those things, just like any new family, so finances were super tight.

I tell you all of this to let you know I know what it's like. I know firsthand people who have financial problems also have health problems. When you're not financially healthy, it's highly unlikely you are going to be physically healthy, mentally healthy, or emotionally healthy. The stress just starts to eat you up.

Many people today have car payments over $1,000 per month. Looking back, not only was I trying to help my clients become financially healthy, but I was also (unknowingly) helping them with their physical, mental, and emotional health as well. Being financially healthy is so important to the rest of your life! Making it a priority is in your best interest.

CHAPTER 10

Financial Wellness and Health are Related.

TABLE 9: FINANCIAL WELLNESS AND HEALTH ARE RELATED

Vulnerable		Coping		Healthy		
Unengaged	At Risk	Striving	Tenuous	Thriving	Focused	Stable
17%		54%		29%		

71% Not Healthy

$

29% Healthy

138 million people are struggling financially

63 million are "underbanked" or "unbanked"

Source: "Study: Majority of Americans Continue to Struggle with Finances." ABA Banking Journal, 2019.

One study found 23 percent of those in debt report having severe depression compared to 4 percent without (table 8). Another study saw a 14 percent increase in depression symptoms with every 10 percent increase in personal debt. Furthermore, 29 percent of those with debt suffer severe anxiety (relative to just 4 percent of those without debt).

There's a Canadian study of lottery winners, and it shows the neighbors of lottery winners were more likely to incur debt and file for bankruptcy. Why's that? Let's just call it keeping up with the Joneses.

If you want to be wealthy, you must avoid this syndrome. It's okay to want to be wealthy, but you've got to get over the obsession with impressing people. The thing is when you pay your house off, you don't get to walk that around the neighborhood and say, *"Hey, look at me! My house is paid up. Oh, I've got a million bucks!"* No, you don't get to do that. And people are more worried about the cars they drive and the clothes they wear.

I am so appreciative that I did not have that gene. I never cared about people "thinking" I was wealthy. I was more driven to "become" wealthy. We always drove a nice car, went on vacations, and had nice homes, but we always lived under our means.

I never wanted to owe people or companies money. We paid off our homes early, we bought our cars with cash, and I own 11 annuities and have a big whole life insurance policy. These are the things many "experts" tell you to stay away from. I can assure you, those "experts" are wrong. I am not just talking the talk; I am walking the walk.

But do you want to know the truth? It's not about looking good. It's about becoming good. It's about becoming wealthy. Feelings of inferiority, feelings of shame, high-risk, self-sabotaging behavior—these are all examples of how your relationship with money can affect your emotional health.

Then there's Alzheimer's and dementia. This is very personal to me. Both of my parents had Alzheimer's. That means I have two Alzheimer's genes myself (I sure hope we get this thing figured out).

Alzheimer's and dementia are associated with adverse financial events starting years before the patient was diagnosed. And those with Alzheimer's or dementia are more likely to miss bill payments up to six years prior to diagnosis.

Why am I telling you all of this? Because it hits close to home (and probably does/will for many readers as well).

For me, I distinctly remember when my sister came in one day and told me our mom was writing all these checks. We asked her what she was doing, and she said, "*Oh, I'm paying all my bills.*" The only problem was there wasn't a single bill on the kitchen table. Not one of them was a bill. They were all requests for money from charities. And what these organizations do is they make their requests look like a bill, and people with dementia or Alzheimer's just write these checks because they are trying desperately to not look like they have a problem.

I'm just telling you if something doesn't seem right financially with your parents, aunts, uncles, or your grandparents, this could be a sign. You're going to be one of the first people that can figure out if somebody has dementia or Alzheimer's.

CHAPTER 11

Taxes are Headed Higher!

TABLE 10: WHERE DO YOU THINK TAX RATES ARE GOING?

- Tax rates are currently at historically low levels, suggesting they may be higher when you retire.

- Tax diversifying your retirement savings may also make sense.

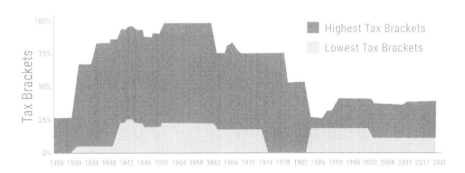

The graph above illustrates the high and low marginal federal income tax rates over history. Exemptions, deductions and state and local taxes are not taken into account when illustrating the marginal tax rates. Your actual tax rates may vary from those shown on the graph. Remember that historical rates are not a guarantee of future rates.

Source: "How Have the Top and Bottom Tax Brackets Changed Over Time?" National Taxpayers Union Foundation, 2021. https://www.ntu.org/foundation/tax-page/how-have-the-top-and-bottom-income-tax-brackets-changed-over-time

Now let's talk about taxes for a moment.

There are three types of taxable investments. There's taxable, tax-deferred, and tax-free. Taxable investments are stocks, bonds, CDs, etcetera. Tax-deferred—which means you don't pay tax until you take money out—includes things like Traditional IRAs, 401(k)s, and annuities. Then there are tax-free investments like Roth IRAs, cash value life insurance, and municipal bonds.

What I think we need to do is really start looking at the tax-free investments because when we go back and study American history, we can clearly see we're living in a time of abnormally low taxes. And it can't stay like this forever.

As a country, we're now over $33 trillion in debt (and climbing at $4 billion every single day). It won't be long before our debt hits $40 trillion on the way to $50 trillion. We have $200 trillion of unfunded obligations for Social Security, Medicare, Medicaid, government pensions, and military pensions. See $33 trillion at 1% interest only costs us $330 billion. But $33 Trillion at 5% interest is $1.5 trillion – almost the entire defense department and Social Security budgets COMBINED! And $50 Trillion at 5% interest is $2.5 trillion. Where is this money going to come from? My question to you is this: *where do you think taxes are going from here* (table 10)?

I'll tell you one thing with complete certainty; taxes are not going down from here. This is not a Republican or Democrat issue—it's a math problem. Taxes must go up—and they're going to have to go up a lot.

See, 30 years ago, when tax rates were higher, 401(k)s made perfect sense. You get a tax deduction going in, the money would grow tax deferred, and when you retired, you were likely in a lower tax bracket. So, you got to get out all of your money and gains (over time) and pay LESS in taxes! What a deal! We all did it.

But does it really make sense to put money in a Traditional 401(k) today? I don't think you should put much into 401(k)s or Traditional IRA's. There's no sense in putting a lot of money into a 401(k) when tax rates are low just so that you can defer all those taxes until ten, twenty, or thirty years into the future when tax rates soar. That makes no sense.

TABLE 11: THE "TAX PERFECT" RETIREMENT PLAN

With proper planning, you can minimize the effect taxes will have on your retirement planning. Ideally, you would be able to create a retirement plan that includes three key attributes:

I always talked to my clients about the importance of tax diversification. Just like you don't want to put all your money in stocks, commodities, or real estate – you want to diversify your investments. The same is true with taxes. You don't want to put all your money in the tax deferred bucket. I'd say something like this:

"You know, the tax-perfect retirement plan would work like this: you get a tax-deductible contribution, it grows tax-deferred, and you get to take the money out tax-free. That would be tax perfect.

"The only problem is this doesn't exist in America. You get to pick one and two, or two and three. You don't get all three. You can pick tax-deductible contributions and grow tax deferred. (that's your IRA, 401(k), or profit sharing). Or you can give up the deduction, but you get tax-deferred accumulation and tax-free income in retirement. That's the Roth IRA and cash value life insurance."

Now, all I'm saying is doesn't it make sense to have money in both buckets? Here's the conversation I would have with a client:

"Does your company have a 401(k)? Yes. Does it offer a match? Yes. Tell me about the match."

They say something like: *"Well, if I put in 4 percent, they give me 4 percent."*

I encourage them to take advantage of that—it's a 100 percent rate of return, after all. However, for anything above the match, I would no longer put it into a Traditional IRA or 401(k). I would put that into a Roth 401(k), Roth IRA, or cash value life insurance.

Beyond the 401(k), start putting that into some place where you can get tax-free income. This is all about tax diversification. When you're building a portfolio, you take advantage of asset allocation and diversification. You also need to be taking advantage of tax diversification.

When I was working with farmers, I would ask them this question: "Would you rather pay tax on the seed or on the harvest?" 100% would say "the seed!" I would say, "exactly! That is the Roth 401(k), Roth IRA, and cash value life insurance." Paying tax on the harvest is what you do with a 401(k) or traditional IRA.

Retirement Income of $100,000

Without Tax Diversification	Tax Diversification Strategy	
$100,000 401 (k) / Qualified Plans	$50,000 401 (k) / Qualified Plans	$50,000[3] Cash Value Life Insurance Roth IRAs, Muni Bonds
100% taxable	100% taxable	Tax free
$100,000 taxed at 25%	$50,000 taxed at 15%[1]	$50,000 taxed at 0%[2]
= $25,000 tax	= $7,500 tax	= $0 tax
$75,000 to spend after taxes	$92,500 to spend after taxes	

Hypothetical example for illustrative purposes only.

1. Assumed marginal federal income tax bracket under current rates.

2. If structured properly, policy loans and partial policy value surrenders will reduce the death benefit of the policy and may cause the life insurance policy to lapse. Distributions exceeding costs basis will result in taxation.

3. The cash value in a life insurance policy is accessed through policy loans, which accrue interest at the current rat and cash withdrawals and loans will decrease the total death benefit and total cash value. Policy values are based or non guarantee factors, such as dividends and interest rates which are subject to change. Therefore the supplemental retirement income is not guaranteed.

CHAPTER 12

Some Tips from Curtis Cloke

urtis V. Cloke, CLTC, LUTCF, RICP is a financial advisor in Burlington, Iowa. His list of accomplishments is impressive. He is a multi-time qualifier of the MDRT's Top of the Table and has trained other financial advisors around the world. I have Curtis do much of my own personal financial planning. He is as good as anyone I know in the entire country around the subject of retirement and retirement income.

What many people don't know is Curtis is also very well versed in almost all investments, to include alternative investments. He is always attending meetings and seminars to learn even more. Curtis and I recently conducted a three-day, six-hour webinar presentation.

- Day 1 was focused on how to become a millionaire.
- Day 2 was our best ideas on how to protect that wealth.
- Day 3 was our best ideas on how to distribute wealth and leave a legacy.

Curtis often talks about how his grandfather had such an impact on him at an early age. Curtis would ride on the tractor at his grandpa's farm, and he learned many basic financial and life values on the knee of his grandfather. Things like:

- How much his grandpa hated debt (You are never really free if you are in debt).
- The importance of giving 10 percent of your earnings to church or charity.
- The importance of saving at least 10 percent of your income (leaving 80 percent of your income to spend).
- When Achieving Success: "Consume Less, Give More & Create More Than You Consume"

In our three-day course, Curtis gave some simple steps to become wealthy.

Step 1 is to develop a Millionaire Mindset. Here are some mindset characteristics that will help you:

- **Planning ahead.** Think ahead about your short-term, medium-term, and long-term financial plan and what you'll do in case of emergencies.
- **Determination.** Know you'll face challenges, but be prepared to overcome them.

- **Patience and delayed gratification.** Be willing to delay present wants for future goals.

- **Confidence.** Have faith in yourself that you can pay off that debt that seems insurmountable, reach that next number in your savings account, or launch the business you've been dreaming about. If you start with the mindset that you can't, you probably won't.

- **Openness.** Be willing to learn, make mistakes (or even fail sometimes), and then learn even more. Seek knowledge and surround yourself with positive influences.

Step 2: Carefully watch your expenses big and small. One of the quickest ways to hamstring your financial progress is to buy too much house or too much car.

You may have heard the term "house poor," and this is what it means. Too many people get caught up in the trap of having overly expensive mortgages and car loans that take up the bulk of their income, leaving them with little or nothing to put toward their savings.

While big purchase decisions only come around occasionally, your financial plan should also account for small expenses. These can be "death by a thousand cuts" to your savings goals. Look for opportunities to reduce costs like your cell phone bill, cable, subscription services, eating out, shopping for non-necessities, and so on.

A great goal is to see if you can live on just half of your income and save the other half. Try it as an experiment for a year and keep it going if you can! This will get you to your million dollars a lot faster.

Step 3: Max out your retirement account contributions. If you max out only your IRA by contributing $500 a month, it will take you about twenty-nine years to become a millionaire. If you max out only your 401(k) by contributing $1,625 a month, it will take you about nineteen years. If you maxed out both accounts for a total of $2,125 a month, you could speed that up to just sixteen years.

My input on that would be to focus on Roth IRAs and Roth 401(k)s if possible. I continue to think tax-free income in retirement is desirable. The problem with regular IRAs and 401(k)s is it is not really your money. You have a partner (the Federal Government). They are the general partner. You are just a limited partner. They get to take their cut first. You get whatever is left over.

The real problem is you have no idea of how much they are going to take when you finally retire. With the incredible amount of government debt on the books, it is nearly guaranteed taxes will be much higher in the future. I think many people will be disappointed to see how little of their IRAs and 401(k)s they will get.

Step 4: Seize any opportunity to increase your income. Of course, it needs to be legal and moral.

- Ask your boss at your current job about opportunities for career growth and promotions.

- Job hunt to see if you can get a higher salary offer for a similar role at a new company.
- Learn new skills to increase your marketability and make a full career change to a more well-paid industry.
- Do side gigs or take on a second job, like work-from-home jobs.
- Start a business, and work to scale it.

Step 5: Use your money to make more money. Most wealthy people don't just sit on a hoard of gold like a dragon—they put their money to work for them. Using your money to make money with little active effort is called "passive income."

The easiest way to generate passive income is by investing in stocks or keeping your savings in high-interest bank accounts. If you manage to max out your retirement accounts for the year, you can continue investing money in a brokerage account or an HSA for health expenses.

Many millionaires attribute their success to real estate investing, which can be active or passive income (depending on your method). There are also some unique ways to make passive income, like purchasing an ATM and earning through fees or owning a vending machine in a well-placed location.

Step 6: This is a tough one: avoid lifestyle creep. As you scale your income, it becomes tempting to scale your lifestyle too. Lifestyle creep happens when items you once considered luxuries are now part of your new normal. This can be as small as buying expensive coffee every morning or as big as buying a beach house or a boat.

Another common trap people fall into is "keeping up with the Joneses."

If your neighbors, friends, and family members are buying nice cars, eating out every day, and upgrading their houses, it's normal for a little jealousy to creep in. But remember, the average American is about $38,000 in debt, not including their mortgages. You don't want to keep up with the Joneses because the Joneses are stressing about how they're going to pay off that BMW.

It might sound a little strange, but to become a millionaire, live like you're the opposite of one.

CHAPTER 13

Final Thoughts

kay, so let me try to bring this in for a landing here. I'll sum it up like this:

- Marriage is hard. Divorce is hard. Choose your hard.
- Obesity is hard. Being fit is hard. Choose your hard.
- Being in debt is hard. Being financially disciplined is hard. Choose your hard.

Life will never be easy. Life is always going to be hard. Choose your hard.

You're not born a winner or a loser. You're born a chooser. Your entire life is a sum of all your choices. Now some of us have made good choices. Others of us have made bad choices, but that doesn't stop us from making good choices in the future.

If you remember nothing else, remember this: you're not a winner, and you're certainly not a loser. You were born a chooser— choose wisely.

I'll leave you with eleven basic tips for financial success that are so boring and sensical that most people trip over them on their way to implement flashy ideas and newfangled techniques.

Some Simple Tips for Financial Success

1. Pay yourself first! Make saving a priority.

2. Invest regularly and automatically.

3. Save at least 15 percent of your income (try to increase to 20 percent as soon as possible).

4. Invest in appreciating assets—you don't get wealthy by putting your money into depreciating assets. Cars, boats, RVs, phones, clothes, shoes, and computers all go down in value every day.

5. Create a budget, and track your expenses.

6. Spend less than what you earn—simplify your life.

7. Establish an emergency fund.

8. Pay off your credit cards; use cash for purchases.

9. Find ways to earn more money.

10. Work with a financial professional.

11. Protect yourself and your family with insurance products.

About the Author

For those of you who don't know me, I want to paint a picture of how my career has led me to this point. I think it'll give you some perspective into why I'm so passionate about helping people with their finances.

I'm originally from a small town in Minnesota (population 2,500—on a good day). I had two younger sisters, and both of my parents were teachers. As you know, teachers in small towns don't exactly make a lot of money. I grew up in a middle-class neighborhood. We had all the necessities but not any luxuries.

I was an excellent student—almost straight A's from high school through college. I wasn't exactly a nerd, but I wasn't one of the "cool kids" either. I also had a tremendous work ethic. From a very young age, I had a propensity to make money. I made money selling seeds door-to-door, flinging newspapers, mowing lawns, shoveling snow, selling candy at the county fair...you name it.

My Army Career

As a kid, I also loved playing "army" with the other neighborhood kids. I had the latest plastic army guns as well as walkie-talkies, plastic knives, grenades—everything an Army man could possibly want. We would dig fox holes, develop attack and defensive strategies, and literally play Army for hours on end. When it came time for college, I applied to West Point and wanted to become a military officer.

Now getting into one of the military academies is very difficult. In fact, it's almost impossible—certainly for me. I had no connections, and my dad never served in the military. You need to be nominated by a member of congress, and as I said, I had zero connections. But I went for the interviews and took the physical fitness tests. While I passed—and they said I was a good candidate—my lack of a nomination kept me out.

At the interview, the Lieutenant Colonel gave me some ROTC Scholarship applications: one for the Army and one for the Navy/Marines. I filled them both out and sent them in.

After receiving an Army ROTC scholarship, I was accepted into four schools. I visited two of the campuses – the University of Minnesota and North Dakota State University. I chose the latter.

The years of 1979 to 1983 were probably the best four of my life. In high school, I was not part of the "in" crowd. I wasn't an outcast—I had many friends—but I wasn't one of the popular ones. At NDSU, however, somehow, I was deemed "cool." I was part of the "in" crowd. In addition to playing lots of intramural football behind Churchill Hall almost every day, I also wound up as the Cadet Battalion Commander (the highest rank you can attain as a cadet).

I wound up earning almost every cadet award on campus my four years, but my greatest prize was meeting my wife, Laurie. I still remember the first time I saw her, and I would tell you the story, but she gets embarrassed. She stole my heart that day. We have now been married forty years and have four kids and three grandchildren.

In May 1983, I graduated from NDSU with three majors— economics, business administration, and German with a minor in military science. I was commissioned as a Second Lieutenant in the US Army. I was also told I was being sent to the 3rd Infantry Division in West Germany.

My years in Germany were tough. I was in an M-1 Tank Battalion holding a Captain's position as a Second Lieutenant. I was a primary staff officer with significant responsibilities. I remember I was only twenty-two years old at the time. I had to deal with superior officers who didn't like Second Lieutenants, Sergeants who were old enough to be my father (or grandfather), and other Lieutenants who were a bit jealous that I had a Captain's position.

After earning an amazing opportunity as a company commander in the 107th Military Intelligence Battalion in the 7th Infantry Division (Light) at Ft. Ord, California and serving there for some time, I eventually reached a point where opportunities outside of the military sounded more appealing.

About this time, there was a MetLife agent who was selling whole life insurance to some of my soldiers. At the time, I was not a believer in cash value life insurance. I bought into the "buy term and invest the difference" mantra so popular in the '80s. I thought he was taking advantage of my soldiers. I told my Sergeant to have him come see me.

When the agent came into my office, I was tough on him. I grilled him about trying to take advantage of my soldiers. He insisted he was doing nothing of the sort. Instead, he was protecting their families, helping them save for their retirement and their children's college education.

He even ran an illustration for me. He got my birthdate from my staff. He showed me a five pay, whole life policy (this was before the 1988 TAMRA, seven pay test was made law). I paid for five years, then stopped. By the sixth year, the policy had a surrender value equal to the total premiums. Every year after that, both the cash value and the death benefit increased. I had never seen anything like it.

If this is true, I asked, why would anyone buy term insurance? He said, "I hardly ever sell any term insurance." I asked him if he got paid to sell these policies. He informed me he was paid very well to sell those policies. I said I could sell those policies! And that is how my career in the financial services industry started.

My career really took off at MetLife, where I learned how to sell and eventually became featured in MetLife magazines. Then the speaking requests came (and that was my foot into the world of public speaking).

I developed a sixty-minute talk about what I did and how I did it. Almost all the managers in the 4 or 5 surrounding states asked me to speak to their advisors. More speaking requests came in.

Soon I was asked to speak on the main platform at a MetLife Leaders Conference in Maui. This was a huge honor. There were probably seven hundred people in the audience—mostly MetLife agents and managers, but quite a few home office people as well. I'm proud of that presentation.

After my presentation, I was approached by some of the home office officers. They needed someone to ignite some excitement into their Variable Universal Life policy. I accepted a position as the National Marketing Manager for Variable Life and decided to really focus on the speaking opportunities and getting variable life sales up.

A few years later MetLife began experiencing some internal turmoil and lawsuits. They were also going from a Mutual Company to a Stock Company. There were many of us not happy with that move. I felt it would hurt our clients. I was approached about an opportunity to join New York Life, and my wife and I jumped at the offer.

When I first started, I had a territory of thirteen states in the Southwest and Central parts of the country. At the time, variable annuities were the rage, and New York Life had some great ones. My territory led the company nearly every year in annuity sales. I was soon promoted to regional manager and eventually national manager. We had an incredible team of annuity wholesalers.

While at New York Life, I really began digging into retirement income and risk management. I got to work with some great company officers. Together we helped refine the products, the messages, and the why behind the what. It all worked, and New York Life soon had a 42 percent market share in income annuities—really something unheard of in an industry with hundreds of companies. However, at the same time, I was once again getting antsy to make a move.

My Busy "Retirement"

When it was clear I would be leaving, I met with a company in Boston working with speakers and authors. They set up my website, helped me with speaking contracts, and helped me get my first book, *Paychecks and Playchecks*, published. Because we had planned all of this in advance, the website was up and running the day I retired from New York Life. Because of the connections I'd made during my time in the industry, numerous people started calling to bring me to train the advisors in their companies. To this day, 100 percent of my speaking engagements are inbound calls.

In my previous books I have talked about my big break speaking at the Boomerretirement Roadshows. That led to invitations to speak at the Top of the Table for MDRT and then in 2010 to the Main Platform at the MDRT Annual Meeting. That is one of the most elite speaking opportunities in the world. I am so thankful to all the people who helped make that happen.

I have now spoken twelve times for MDRT—all over the world—to include Singapore, Taiwan, Thailand, and Australia. In 2013, I spoke on the main platform for GAMA.

In 2014, PBS approached me to do a PBS TV Special based on my latest book at that time—*Don't Worry, Retire Happy*. It was a big success, and that book has now surpassed *Paychecks and Playchecks* in sales.

For the past eleven years or so, I have continued to be on the road two-hundred-plus days a year, training advisors and conducting public seminars for their clients and prospects. Traveling that much is grueling. You can't remember what room you're in or what kind of car you are driving—the marathon effect of it all is draining. I have really felt it in the last couple of years. Which takes us to my trial retirement.

Life has started looking a bit more precious to me in recent years. I lost my best golfing buddy and one of my very best friends five years ago. He was fifty-six. Two years ago, I lost my dad. Then I lost my mom. Recently I lost a forty-one-year-old friend to COVID.

You start to see there are no guarantees in your life. I have no desire to be the richest guy in the cemetery. I tell people all the time, *"You're not getting any younger, and you don't get to take any of it with you!"* Read that a few more times. Well, I sat down, looked at my financial situation, and realized I could do this. I am now living exactly what I have been preaching for years.

I own eleven annuities and have four pensions. Both my wife and I have long-term care insurance policies. We also bought a life insurance policy for the kids so we can spend all our money. I have done exactly what the PhDs I have studied have said I should do. So, I began asking myself, why am I still sleeping in four different hotel rooms every single week? That is NOT what I want to do. Yes, I still love speaking in front of a crowd, but I don't like all the stuff I need to do to get there and back.

Time to Go Virtual

In late 2018 or early 2019, I attended a meeting of the National Speakers Association. I am part of a special group called the Million Dollar Speakers Group. This is basically the top thirty to forty speakers in the world. All of them make over a million dollars a year from speaking. I can tell you I am a minnow in this incredible group, but I have learned so much from them.

One session focused on how to drive revenue from webinars and other virtual sources. They showed how you could make money without traveling 200 days a year. I was hooked! I spent the next 6 months transforming my business to the virtual world.

Then, in 2020, COVID-19 hit the world. Everything was turned upside down. My speaking revenue went to zero. The financial services industry was reeling. Advisors couldn't meet face-to-face with clients and prospects. All seminars and training meetings were canceled. Things looked grim.

Well, as I said, I had been preparing for zero revenue (i.e. my retirement). I had been moving things to the cloud and had created multiple "evergreen webinars."

Well, guess what? Those webinars worked. Immediately I was seeing revenue come in every day from these webinars. I also quickly moved into the live webinar space. Companies hired me to do webinars to train their advisors and educate their clients and prospects.

Because I didn't have to travel, I could literally do five or six webinars in a day instead of one or two live seminars per day. I could work for four or five companies in a day instead of one company. I soon found I could be much more efficient in this new virtual world. I developed new content to help advisors thrive in this lockdown and post-lockdown environment. My revenue spiked. I was one of the only people in the industry ready to go on day one of this whole COVID thing. I was surprised I had more virtual capacity than several Fortune 500 companies.

My phone started ringing off the hook. Companies were frantically trying to help their advisors stay in business. I was doing five, six, and sometimes up to eight webinars per day.

We built a small house in Flagstaff, Arizona where we spend our summers. But the house was too small for me to do all these webinars. I couldn't kick the family out of the house every time I did a webinar. I actually had to rent an office in 2020—just for my webinars!

We now have a bigger home in Flagstaff, so I have a dedicated office for that.

I am now mostly retired. I play golf 4 to 5 days a week. I play pickleball 2 days a week. My wife and I are travelling the world and getting along better than we ever have. Life is fun! As I said earlier in the book, I'm a golfer. For 30 years I could not make the numbers work for joining a country club. I was travelling so much I could maybe play 3 or 4 times a month.

When I looked at the buy-in cost, the monthly dues, and the minimum food and beverage requirement, it made no financial sense. Today? I'm a member at 2 Country Clubs! One up in Flagstaff where we spend our summers and one in Mesa where we spend our winters. Best of all, the numbers make great sense since I'm playing so much golf.

Better yet, in 2020, I won the Club Championship at Flagstaff Ranch! For me, that was beyond belief. In 2022, I won the Senior Club Championship and my wife and I won the Couples Net Club Championship. I feel like I'm at summer camp every day. And that is what I want for you as well. Whatever you envision for your retirement, I wish you much happiness and success!